Face Painting

Jacqueline Russon

Contents

CollinsChildren'sBooks

First things first

Next time you're having a party, going out for the day or want to surprise someone, why not paint your face? Once you've tried the ten faces in the book, try making up your own.

All you need is ...

Using a sponge

Wet the sponge. Squeeze it to get rid of the water. Wipe it around the paint pot and then gently dab the face. Sponge the eyes last. Make sure they are closed.

Using a brush

Wet the brush and then dip it into the paint. Take care. If it is too wet, the paint will run. If it is too dry, it will pull on the skin.

Blending

Blending is a way of mixing two colours together. Sponge on one colour first. Let it dry. Gently rub on the second colour with a dry sponge or your fingers.

Cuddly teddy

Why not have a teddy bear's picnic?

1 Sponge the face yellow all over. Blend reddish brown around the outside. Dab a little red on the cheeks.

2 Paint the tip of the nose and a curly mouth in black. Add little black whisker spots.

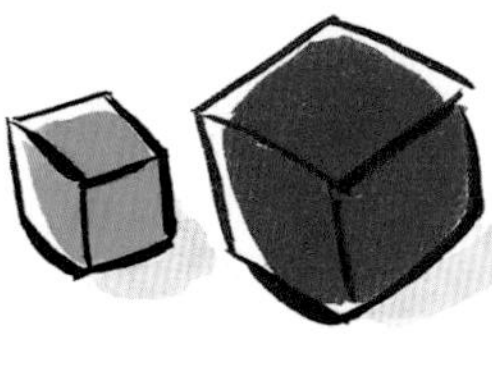

The colours you need are...

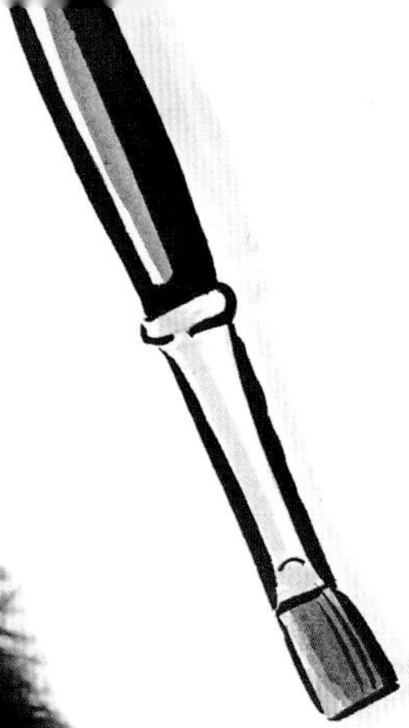

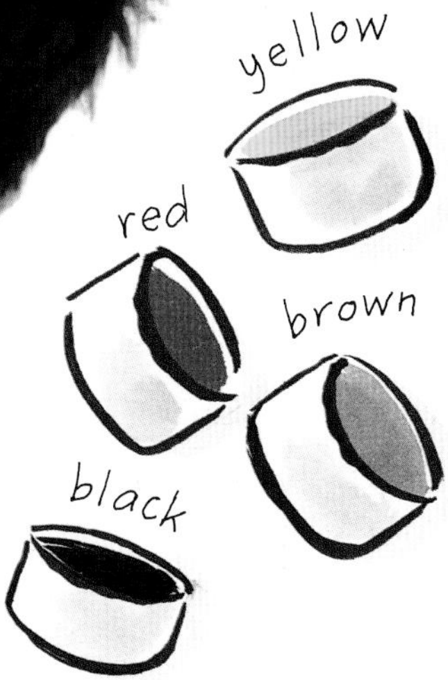

3 Paint a black circle around the eyes and two little black eyebrows on the forehead.

Cheery clown

Turn somersaults and play some tricks!

1 Paint a huge red smiley mouth. Sponge a red spot on the nose.

The colours you need are...

2 Carefully paint brightly coloured stripes over the eyelids. Add pointed black eyebrows over the stripes.

3 Sponge bright green spots on to the cheeks. Paint multi-coloured dots above them.

Scary ghost

Here's a spooky face for Hallowe'en.

1 Paint a white ghost shape over the face, like this.

2 Add a large black patch over each eye and another one over the nose.

The colours you need are...

3 Carefully colour the rest of the face black. Paint wobbly green eyebrows above the eye patches.

Mini monster

Mind you don't frighten the neighbours!

1 Paint a large yellow circle around both eyes. Paint a pattern of bright green scales on the forehead, nose, cheeks and chin.

2 Fill in the rest of the face with purple. Paint the lips dark red.

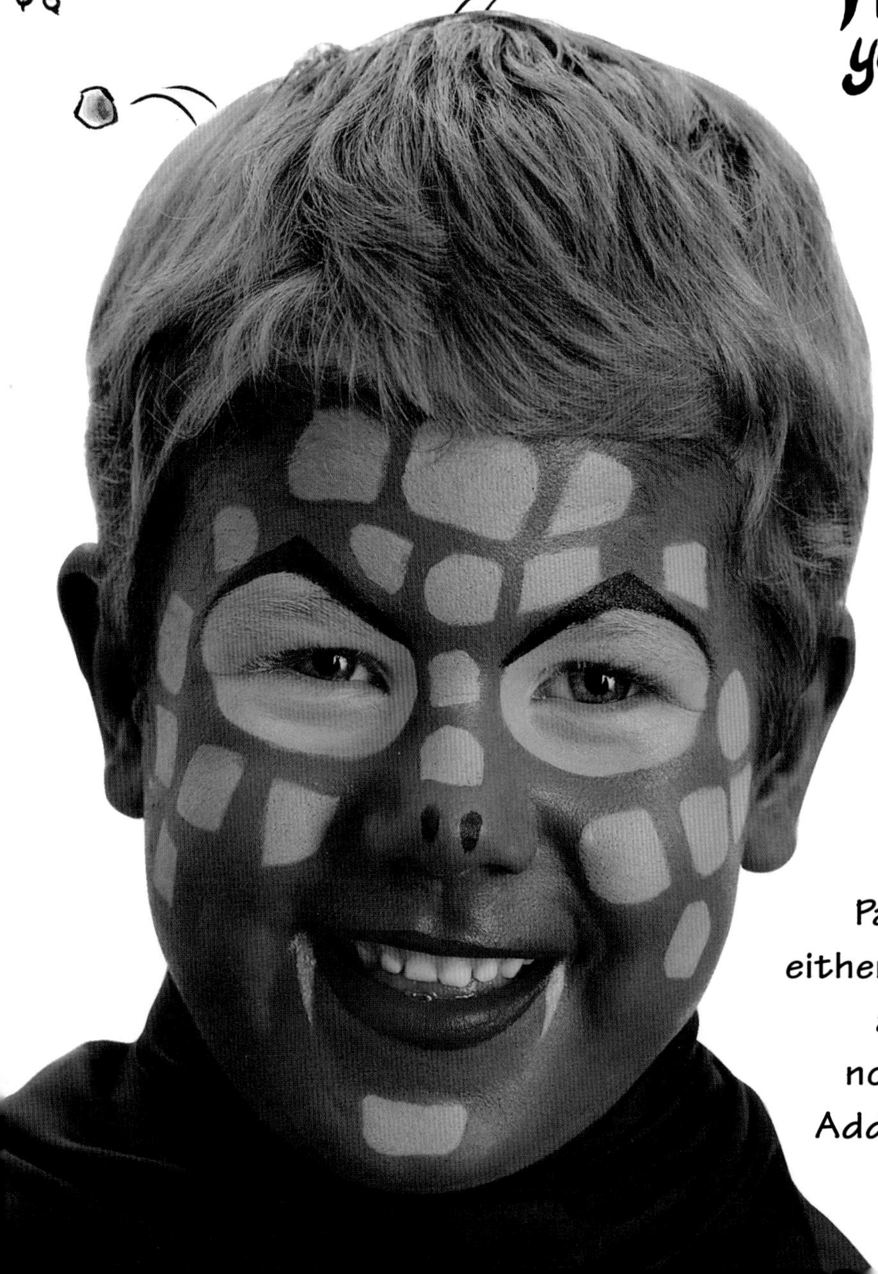

The colours you need are...

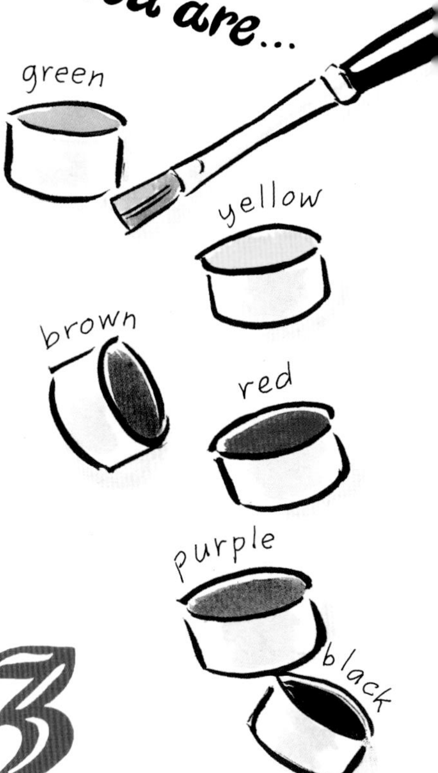

3

Paint white fangs on either side of the mouth and two little black nostrils on the nose. Add pointed eyebrows.

Funny bunny

Practise twitching your nose like a real rabbit.

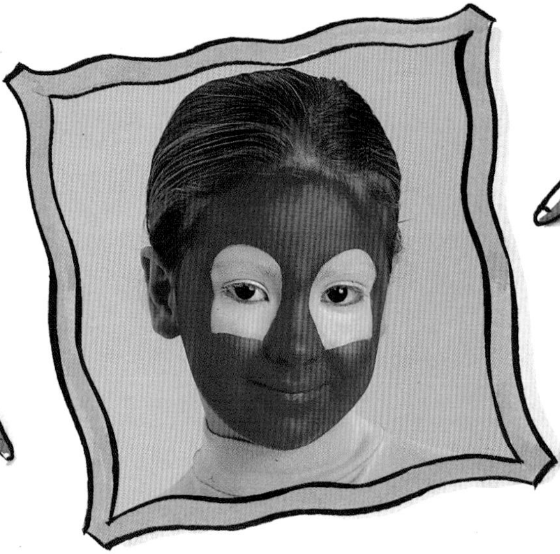

1 Sponge dark pink over the whole face. Paint a pale pink arch over each eye.

2 Paint a grey feathery muzzle. Draw white teeth over the top and bottom lip. Leave to dry.

The colours you need are...

3 Paint black eyebrows over the arches and add a black nose and whiskers.

Outline the teeth in black as well.

Shiny robot

Walk with stiff arms and legs just like a robot.

The colours you need are...

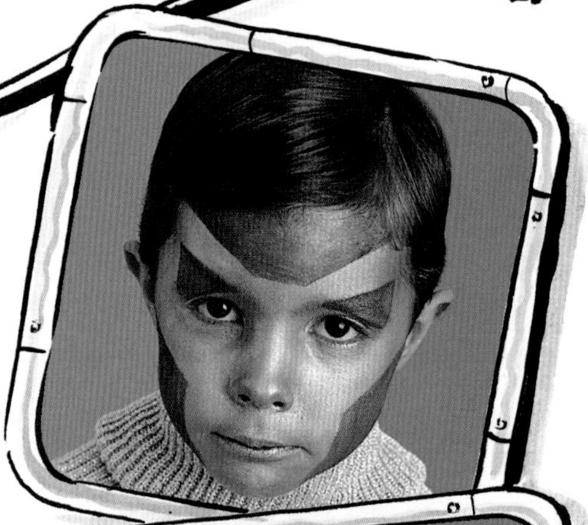

1 Colour the whole face silver. Paint dark grey panels on the cheeks and forehead and triangles over the eyebrows.

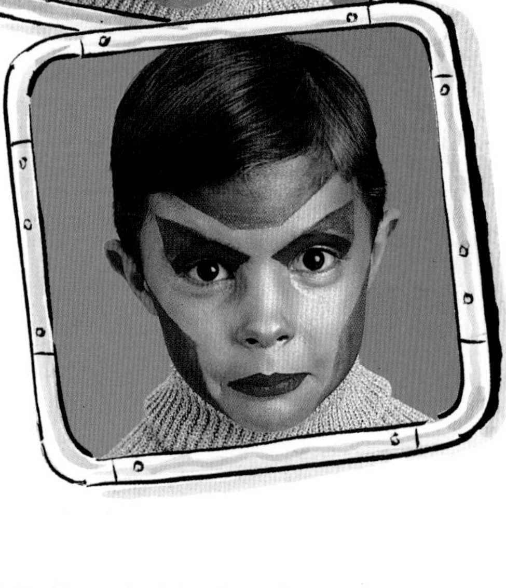

2 Paint the lips and the eyelids bright red.

Tie silver material around the head to complete the effect.

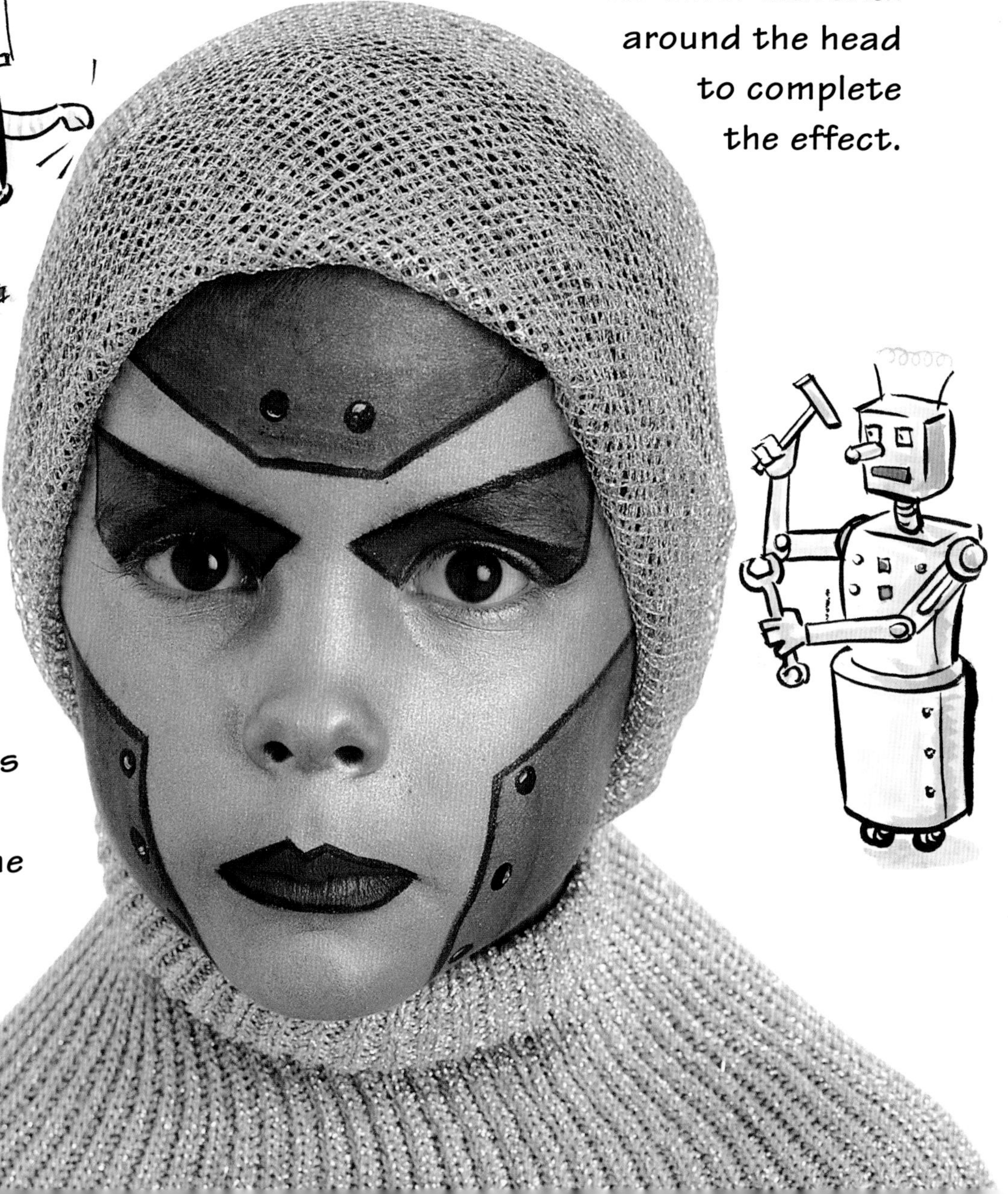

3

Outline the lips and shapes in black. Paint black screws with white flecks on the panels.

Stripy cat

Prowl around the garden with this furry face.

1 Sponge yellow all over the face. With a finger, rub red and brown around the edges and white around the mouth. Paint bushy white eyebrows.

2 Paint red, brown and black stripes all around the outside of the face. Make long stripes on the forehead.

The colours you need are...

3 Backcomb the hair to make it look wild and furry.

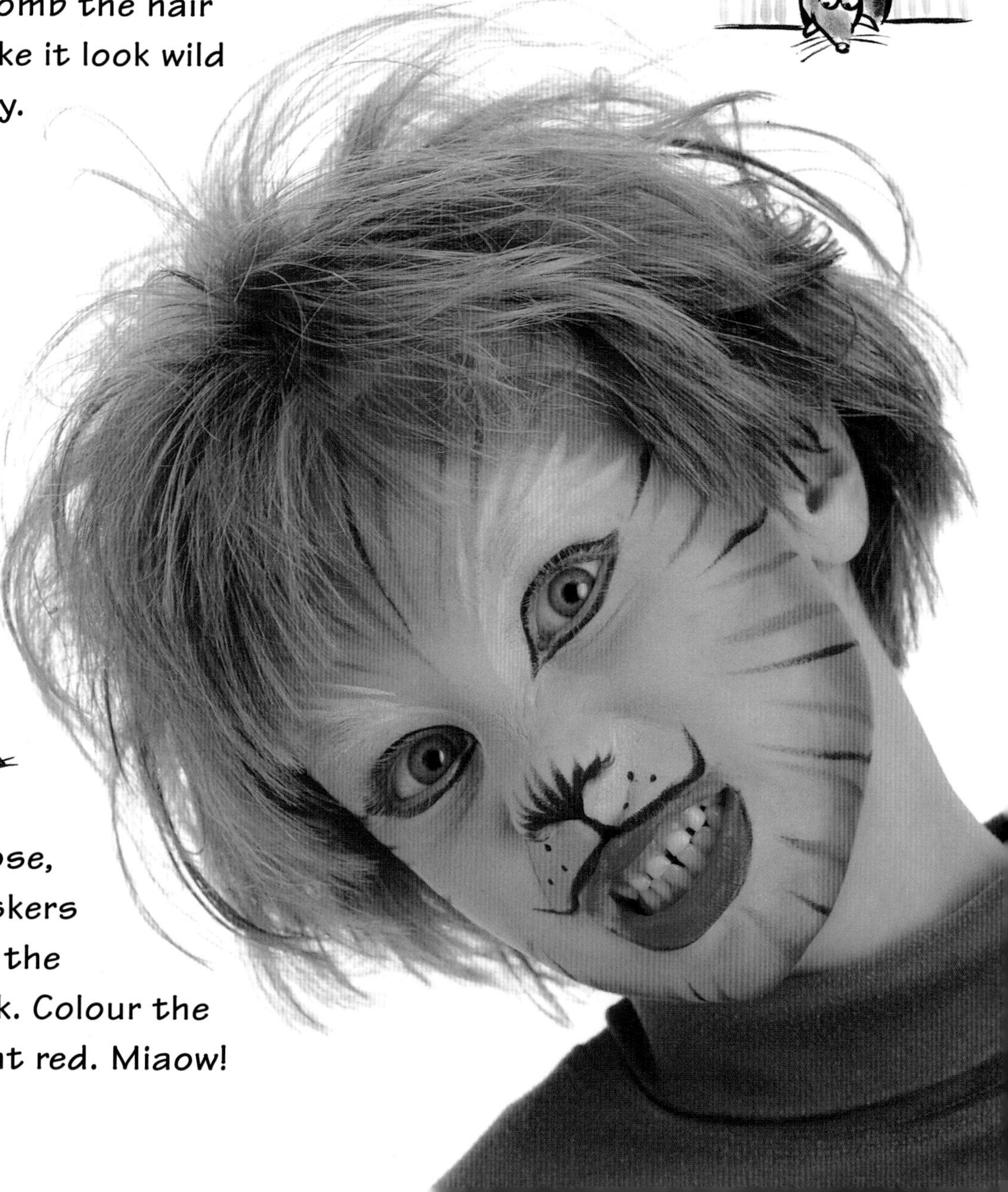

Paint the nose, mouth, whiskers and around the eyes in black. Colour the mouth bright red. Miaow!

Watery mermaid

Decorate your hair with shells and sing sweetly!

1 Paint a green wavy base over part of your face, leaving a shell shape over each eye. Fill in the rest with white foamy waves.

2 Carefully paint pink, silver and purple striped shells over the eyelids and eyebrows. Blend the colours together.

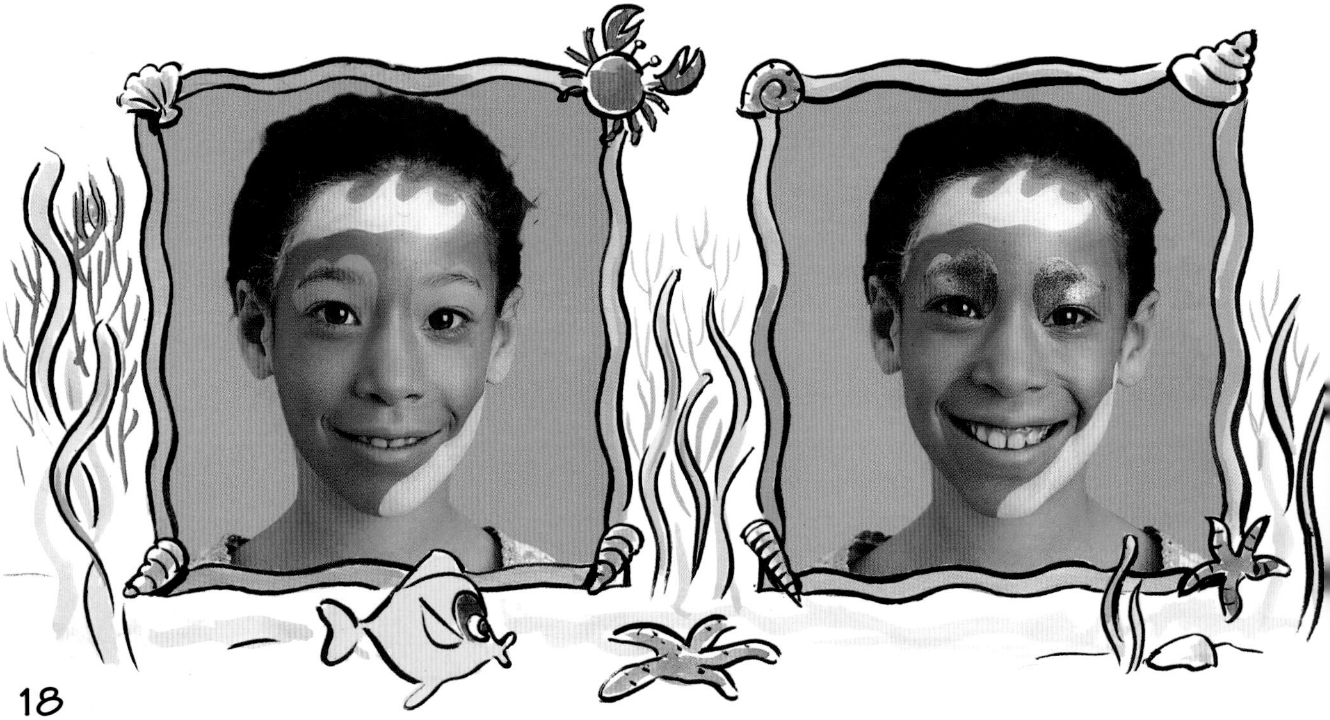

3 Sponge pink spots on to the cheeks. Paint the lips purple.

The colours you need are...

green
white
pink
purple
silver

Spotty dog

Would you give this doggie a bone?

1 Sponge the face white. Paint black patches around both eyes. Dab smudgy spots on the chin, cheeks and forehead.

2 Carefully paint a black nose tip and mouth. Add several black whisker spots.

The colours you need are...

3 Paint a bright red tongue hanging out of the mouth and black eyebrows.

If you have long hair, tie it in bunches to make it look like long doggy ears. Woof!

Pretty Polly

You'll really stand out with this face!

1 Paint a yellow beak over the nose. Add dark green feather shapes on the forehead, eyebrows and cheeks.

2 Add some red feathers. Paint red over the eyelids and put a red nostril on either side of the nose.

The colours you need are...

3

Paint purple and orange feathers in between the red and green ones.

Index

Edited by Ruth Thomson
Designed by Mei Lim

First published in 1996 by HarperCollins Children's Books,
A Division of HarperCollins Publishers Ltd,
77-85 Fulham Palace Road, London W6 8JB

ISBN: 0 00 197937 X

Illustrations : Mei Lim
Photographs : Steve Shott

A CIP record for this book is available from the British Library

Printed and bound in Hong Kong